IMAGES
of America

CONWAY

COL. A.P. ROBINSON, THE FATHER OF CONWAY. Robinson, chief engineer of the Little Rock and Fort Smith Railroad, put Conway on the map when he chose a section of land (payment from the railroad for services rendered) to establish a town. Robinson fenced 320 acres of the land for his plantation, Prairie Vue, and built his home facing what is now College Avenue. Locally, Robinson served as a councilman, mayor, and president of the public school board. The photo was taken in 1910.

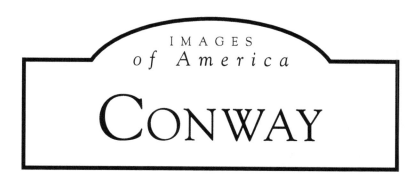

IMAGES
of America

CONWAY

Ann Newman

ARCADIA
PUBLISHING

Published by Arcadia Publishing
Charleston, South Carolina

Library of Congress Catalog Card Number: Applied for

For all general information contact Arcadia Publishing at:
Telephone 843-853-2070
Fax 843-853-0044
E-mail sales@arcadiapublishing.com
For customer service and orders:
Toll-Free 1-888-313-2556

Visit us on the Internet at www.arcadiapublishing.com

CONTENTS

THE SECOND FAULKNER COUNTY COURTHOUSE IN 1893. This building replaced the first courthouse, which burned in 1890.

ACKNOWLEDGMENTS

In 2000 Conway will celebrate its 125th year as an incorporated town. However, Conway's history actually covers over 129 years, with the arrival of the railroad in 1870. Through these years, Conway has continued to grow but has retained its small-town atmosphere. Traditional Southern hospitality remains, thanks to the many people who call Conway, Arkansas, home.

The author gratefully acknowledges the support of the University of Central Arkansas Archives, Director of Archives and Special Collections Jimmy Bryant and his staff members, and the Faulkner County Historical Society, who compiled and published *Faulkner County: Its Land and People.*

I would also like to thank W.C. Jameson for suggesting the project; Jeffrey J. Lutonsky; Hazel Devera, for scanning my images; and Tommy J. Ingram for technical assistance. Special thanks to my husband, Rick, and my children, Rick, Adam, Beth, and Cassie, for their moral support throughout this project.

Finally, acknowledgments need to be made to those who have worked so hard to preserve the heritage of Conway. Among those are the Faulkner County Historical Society, the Faulkner County Museum Board, and the City of Conway.

INTRODUCTION

The year 1870 found Conway Station a small frontier settlement growing around a newly built railroad depot. Some people say that the community was named for the Conway family, which generated two Arkansas governors, while others think it was named for the Little Rock & Fort Smith Locomotive Conway. A third possibility is that the settlement was named for Conway County, the county in which it was located at the time.

On July 6, 1871, one square mile encompassing Conway Station was deeded to Asa P. Robinson, chief engineer of the Little Rock and Fort Smith Railroad, for the sum of $2,994, which was owed to him for services rendered to the railroad. Robinson had planted cotton and begun subdividing the property into lots to establish "his" town one year earlier. Still committed to the railroad project, Robinson had little time to develop Conway Station in its budding years.

News of the railroad station brought men with dreams. Max Frauenthal, a German immigrant, arrived in Conway Station with railroad construction crews in 1871 and saw opportunity. Frauenthal built a small wooden mercantile, the new settlement's second store, in 1872. He chose a lot along the alley, across from the town square and Railroad Avenue where farmers left their wagons in order to have first shot at their business. The alley later became Front Street. (Frauenthal's store was located at the south end of what is now American Management Corporation.)

Settlers established churches shortly after arriving at Conway Station. First United Methodist Church, First Baptist Church (which began with 17 people), and St. Joseph Church (which began with the Joseph Schichtl family) were organized by 1873.

When Faulkner County was formed on April 12, 1873, by combining parts of Conway and Pulaski Counties, Conway Station was selected as the county seat because of the railroad depot, setting the gears into motion for rapid growth. A.P. Robinson donated property for the first courthouse, which is the site of the courthouse still used today.

On October 5, 1875, 30 citizens petitioned to incorporate Conway as a town, dropping "Station" from the name. Max Frauenthal's mercantile continued to prosper, and in 1875 he brought in a cousin, Jo Frauenthal, to help. A year later, another cousin, Leo Schwartz, arrived from Germany to work in the store.

Conway was taking shape: platform walkways lined the wooden shops and businesses. Large signs atop the stores displayed the owner's names. A fire in 1878 changed everything. In a matter of minutes, every store on Front Street burned to the ground. Businessmen scrambled to replace their stores. Frauenthal, ever the leader, erected Conway's first brick building in 1879. The building was fronted with a plate-glass window, also a "first" in Conway.

Able F. Livingston founded the *Conway Log Cabin* (now the *Log Cabin Democrat*) in 1879. The newspaper was published as a republican paper until J.W. Underhill assumed control in the late 1880s. J.W. Robins took ownership in 1894, and the paper remained in the Robins family until 1994.

Early education in Conway was conducted in two private schools: the Lorentz residence and a parochial school operated by St. Joseph's congregation. On October 3, 1878, a group of citizens formed Conway School District No. 1 and elected Joe Van Ronkle as president of the new school board. A five-mill property tax was levied to raise funds to build a school and pay teachers' salaries. Businessmen and citizens contributed money and labor to the project, and in 1879 Conway's first public school, the Little Green Building, was built on six lots (at the north end of Locust Street) donated by A.P. Robinson.

Farming was important to Conway. Cotton was "the crop" in Faulkner County. Farmers from all over the county brought their cotton bales to market in Conway. Wagon yards sprang up all over town with as many as 12 in operation at once. The facilities provided a place to park wagons, stalls for horses, mules, and oxen, bunkhouses for women and men. Feed for the animals and food for the patrons were usually brought from home. The large structures could accommodate 15 to 100 wagons.

The wagon yards were filled from August through March. The trip to the cotton market was an exciting adventure for the farmer's family. Most visited the Crystal Theater to view a picture show. Back at the wagon yard, everyone talked about the movie into the night. Some ate at restaurants and sampled new food. Friends were made, and news and stories exchanged. Often, a year's worth of provisions was purchased before returning home.

By 1880 Frauenthal's mercantile had grown so much that he formed a partnership with Jo Frauenthal. The mercantile became M. and J. Frauenthal & Company. Much of Frauenthal's business was conducted by extending credit to farmers. He held chattel mortgages on their property and belongings against the goods they purchased. The practice made the M. and J. Frauenthal Company large landowners. The company eventually expanded to include a group of businesses: gins, a cotton press, portable engines, mills, and a factory.

Saloons were among the early businesses to open in Conway. E.C. Dunlap opened the Billard Saloon at Front and Oak Streets, perhaps as early as 1873. Another was located east of the depot. By 1888 the number of licensed saloons rose to six. The establishments caused much controversy among local citizens. Methodist minister Edward A Tabor led a group of residents in an effort to close them. Using the "three-mile law," which prohibited the sale of liquor within 3 miles of a public school, the Faulkner County Circuit Court ordered the saloons closed by the end of business December 31, 1888.

In 1892 Max Frauenthal sold his interest in the mercantile to Jo Frauenthal and Leo Schwarz. The store was renamed Frauenthal and Schwarz. Max Frauenthal, compared to the Rockefellers and Vanderbilts on a small-town scale, was and still is an important businessman in the early entrepreneurial history of Conway.

Higher education came to Conway in 1890 when Hendrix College (purchased by the Methodist Church) was relocated from Altus, Arkansas. Central Baptist College for Women followed in 1892, and Arkansas State Normal (now the University of Central Arkansas) in 1907. By the early 20th century, Conway had electricity, a water system, the Conway Telephone Exchange, a fire station, a bank, a post office, more churches, and a newspaper laying a strong foundation for future industry. Conway had become a good place to call home.

One

BUSINESS

Men with dreams of a prosperous future arrived in Conway, eager to make a fresh start. Hard work and generosity built the foundation of a town that would continue to grow without losing its sense of community.

THE HOTEL DE HINES, THE EARLIEST DOCUMENTED HOTEL IN CONWAY. Built by Andrew J. Horton in 1874–75 on the corner of Parkway and Main Streets, this hotel was first known as the Conway Hotel and was sometimes referred to as the Horton Hotel. The notorious Belle Starr and her daughter Pearl lived at the hotel for six months in 1876 while visiting a cousin at Holland. The hotel changed owners and names several times before it burned in 1920.

THE ERBACHER BROTHERS MEAT MARKET, 303 NORTH FRONT STREET. An advertisement in the 1924 Conway Telephone Directory read as follows: "Brothers John and Will Offer Quality Choice Fresh and Cured Meats—Fish and Game In Season—Quality, We Have It—Service, We Give It—Satisfaction, We Guarantee It." The business had two phone numbers: 90 and 91.

THE ERBACHER BROTHERS MEAT MARKET. A second advertisement in the 1924 Conway Telephone Directory read as follows: "John and Bill (Will must also go by Bill) Your Butchers— Choice Fresh and Cured Meats—We Have Our Own Ice Plant—Our Meats Are Properly Cold Storaged—We buy Fat Cattle and Hogs, Veal Calves, Poultry and Eggs—See Us Before You Sell—Milk Cows Bought, Sold and Exchanged." The installation of a glass showcase gave customers an opportunity to view pre-cut meat.

MEN CONGREGATE IN A LOCAL SALOON, 1888. Gambling rooms were located in the back of the establishment. At the close of business on December 31, 1888, all saloons in Conway were permanently closed. In 1935 liquor was again sold in Conway, in several cafes and a newsstand. In 1943, with a vote of 1,753 to 488, the county went dry. It remains dry to this day.

THE CURETON DRUGSTORE, 1904. Dr. Hugh Eli Cureton and C.H. Nelson, a store clerk, are shown here in the Cureton Drugstore. Dr. Cureton opened his store in February 1903.

THE MCKASKLE BLACKSMITH SHOP. Known as Uncle Bill, W.F. McKaskle (in blacksmith's apron and beard) and his brother, D.C. McKaskle, helped with the iron work when Old Main at Central College (now Central Baptist College) was built. The business was believed to be located near Mill Street, between the railroad tracks and Clifton Street. The photo was taken in 1900.

WORKERS PREPARE TO OPEN THE MEAT MARKET IN THE J.A. BOYDSTON STORE, 1904. The ledger on the right suggests that the store offered customers a line of credit.

S.G. SMITH'S GENERAL STORE, FRONT AND NORTH STREETS. Smith, a prosperous businessman, also ran a cotton sale barn. The photo was taken in 1906.

A 1908 Interior View of an Unidentified General Store.

The Boydston General Store, Center Street. This photo was also taken in 1908.

CASPER DUNN'S BAKERY IN 1910. A Main Street brochure advertised this as being "Used by Conway's most discriminative citizens." A dedicated force of employees were needed to carry out his orders.

I.N. FIELDS' FIRST BLACKSMITH SHOP. This photo was taken in 1910.

HARVEY'S NICKLE STORE, 1919. James Francis (Jim) Harvey owned this store and several others in the county until his death in 1934. The store pictured here was located near what is now Haven's Furniture Mart on Highway 64 West. The man standing on the porch is believed to be J.H. Havens.

WORKINGMAN'S RESTAURANT. Workers pose with customers in 1920.

WORKINGMAN'S RESTAURANT, 1920.

THE FRAUENTHAL AND SCHWARZ GENERAL STORE, FRONT STREET, 1923. Pictured from left to right are Arthur Pierce, Chester Markham, Coy Parker, and Emmitt Witt. Jo Frauenthal and Leo Schwarz, owners of the store, bought the prosperous mercantile from their cousin, Max Frauenthal, in 1892. The business closed in 1952.

I.N. FIELDS' BLACKSMITH SHOP. Men pose with equipment used to build wagons in 1920.

THE I.N. FIELDS AND SON BLACKSMITHS AND WAGONMAKERS SHOP, 1920.

HAMIL'S CORNER, Donaghey and Bruce Street, 1924. College students frequented this store.

The King Motel, Highway 64 West. This was Faulkner County's first motel. Ida and Dewey Wofford built a service station with living quarters and a short-order cafe in 1933. They built three double-unit cabins a short time later.

OLSEN'S MUSIC STORE, 1955. Jasper "Jap" Olsen opened this store on Front Street in 1942. The business is currently located on Prince Street.

THE WILL MATTISON BLACKSMITH SHOP, 1955. Willie Mattison opened his business at the corner of Markham and Mill Streets in 1903. Courtney Mattison, Will Mattison's nephew, now owns the business known as Mattison's Shop.

Two

INDUSTRY AND SERVICE

In 1896 Conway had a gristmill, two cotton gins, a planing mill, a harness factory, a harrow factory, a cotton-seed oil mill, and a sash, a door, and a blind factory. Each year brought more people with ideas and talents eager to offer their services to a growing population.

THE LOG CABIN NEWSPAPER OFFICE, 1890S. From left to right are O.C. Ludwig, Milly Burns, W.M. Carr, Frank Robins, Mrs. Carr, Hattie Myrick, and Will Farmer. Able F. Livingston founded the newspaper in 1879 as *The Conway Log Cabin*. J.W. Robins traded his sawmill operation for the newspaper to provide an educational atmosphere for his 13-year-old son, Frank. The Robins family owned the newspaper until 1994.

THE BANK OF CONWAY. When the Bank of Conway was established on April 29, 1890, at 908 Front Street, customers were able to bank locally rather than travel to Little Rock for their banking needs. George W. Donaghey, a carpenter (and later governor of Arkansas), built the bank. The project was his first major construction job.

THE RYE-OLA BOTTLING WORKS, NORTH FRONT STREET. In the center is Leigh Rotton, and to the right is Lee Moe, a Chinese laundry man who has dropped in for a drink. Rev. J.C. Dawson owned the company, which bottled a beverage that tasted similar to Coca-Cola. This photo was taken in 1905.

A LUMBER YARD. Workmen pose with equipment in 1910.

THE CENTRAL BROOM COMPANY, 1913. Established in 1912, the company made 1,200 dozen brooms a month in addition to brushes and mops.

THE CONWAY POST OFFICE, FRONT STREET, 1920. Postal clerks pose in the mailroom. The main post office was relocated to Conway from Cadron Gap in 1872.

CONWAY'S FIRST BRICK FIRE STATION. This building was constructed in 1917 at Prairie Street, where the Conway Corporation building is now located. Pictured from left to right are M.C. Turner, Rod Dickerson (fire chief), several unidentified children, Doss B. Wright (light plant engineer), and E.V. Leverett (plant superintendent.)

THE ELECTRICAL PLANT, 1920. Located at the present site of the Conway Corporation's office building, this plant contained Conway's first steam generator. Professor George Hutchinson Burr (far right), vice-president of the Conway Electric and Manufacturing Company (which was incorporated in July 1895), designed and operated the electric plant and distribution system. When the plant first went into operation, electricity was only supplied between sundown and midnight.

CONWAY'S FIRST RADIO STATION, KFKQ (KNOWN FOR KNOWLEDGE QUEST.) This station first went on the air in 1923. Its programs usually aired on Tuesday and Friday nights, but only if Mr. Woodruff (a college-aged man) was around.

27

A LUMBER YARD. Men are shown posed with horse-drawn machinery in 1925.

THE SOUTHWESTERN BELL TELEPHONE EXCHANGE, 1925. Southwestern Bell bought the Conway Telephone Exchange, developed by Professor George Hutchinson Burr, in late 1911.

THE FAULKNER COUNTY DAIRY COMPANY. Formerly known as the Faulkner County Cooperative Cream Station, this company was formed in 1924 to raise stock for expansion. A new plant was constructed on Harkrider Street in 1926. Shown here, from left to right, are B.H. Hawk, Rector White, R.L. Wilson, Robert Wilson, Rip Gooch, and Russell Johnson. The machine seen on the left made ice cream.

A VIEW OF THE COTTON OIL MILL ON MILL STREET, 1930. The mill is represented by the tall stacks on the right; the Bob Adams Gin is the building on the far left. The gin burned in 1937 and was never rebuilt.

29

THE FEDERAL COTTON COMPRESS COTTON YARD. Note the wooden racks used to store cotton off the ground. This photo was taken in 1930.

AN EARLY SINCLAIR GAS STATION, 1935.

A WORK CREW AT THE WARD BUS BODY SHOP POSES IN FRONT OF A COMPLETED BUS, 1936.
Dave Ward (third from the left) began building school bus bodies in his blacksmith shop on
Harkrider Street in 1934. At one time the bus company was the largest industry in Faulkner
County. The company is now called the AmTran Corporation.

THE JOHN HESS MACHINE SHOP.

WOMEN AT WORK IN THE COOPERATIVE CANNING KITCHEN, 1941. Ethel Millar and Mrs. Wellington Robbins managed the project organized by the Good Will Association in the 1930s to help people help themselves.

THE OTIS MOORE GIN, 1945. Otis Moore built this gin in 1934 on what is now the site of Fred's Discount. Moore and his son, J.O. Moore Jr., operated the gin until the mid-1960s. The man on the right in this photograph is Faber Padgett.

YOUNG BOYS PLAY AROUND COTTON BALES AT THE ENDERLIN AND SEITER GIN (MURRAY'S GINS) AT 1014 MARKHAM STREET, 1945. The boy on the right is Joseph Seiter. In 1929 Joseph Enderlin and Charlie Seiter bought the first Otis Moore Gin. Enderlin retired in 1937, giving his half of the partnership to his sons, Henry and Paul. The Enderlin brothers bought Seiter's interest in 1953 and changed the name to the Enderlin Brothers Gin. The gin baled the last of the cotton baled in Faulkner County before closing in 1972.

A WORKER RELAXES IN THE DOORWAY OF THE OTIS MOORE GIN, 1945. At one time more than 20 gins were in operation in Faulkner County.

THE CONWAY POST OFFICE, 1949.

THE OLD CONWAY HOSPITAL, 1964. J.E. Little donated land at the corner of College and Western Avenue for Conway's first hospital. Construction of the 33-bed facility began in 1923.

Three

STREET SCENES

A handful of wooden buildings sprang up around Conway Station in 1870, establishing the birth of a town that would continue to grow and change. Each business, church, school, and home carries with it a piece of history and a legacy of Conway.

A VIEW OF CONWAY, LOOKING UP EAST STREET, IN 1910.

A View of Front and Oak Street, Looking North, in 1900.

The Second Saint Joseph Catholic Church, 1945. The Joseph Schichtl family established Saint Joseph Parish in 1873. (The first church was completed and blessed in 1879.) Father Wilms, the first resident priest, constructed the first church (destroyed by a storm in 1883) on property that the Missouri Pacific Railroad made available through grants.

THE FIRST BAPTIST CHURCH, 1908. Founded as Conway Baptist Church in 1871, the church building located on Van Ronkle Street was built and dedicated in March 1876. A storm destroyed the building in 1883. Construction of a new church began on May 28, 1885, at the corner of Caldwell and Faulkner Streets.

A TYPICAL SCENE AT THE COTTON MARKET, FRONT STREET, 1909. Cotton buyers are shown standing along the sidewalks. To the far left is the intersection of Front and Oak Streets. The two-story building to the right is Frauenthal and Schwarz. Town hall was located on the second floor of the store during the 1880s. Dances, balls, skating, and other social functions were held there.

DOWNTOWN FLOODING, 1910. Dr. J.Z. Bailey (left) and John Dunaway are shown standing on a railroad loading platform at Railroad (later renamed Parkway) Avenue while surveying the

flood damage to downtown Conway.

A STREET SCENE, LOOKING NORTH FROM FRONT STREET, 1909. The streets would soon fill with farmers eager to sell their cotton bales and attend the first Faulkner County Fair.

THE FIRST METHODIST EPISCOPAL CHURCH, CLIFTON AND PRINCE STREETS, 1910. THE First Methodist Church was established in the early 1870s. The Little Red Church, razed in 1915 to build the present church, was the congregation's third building.

A VIEW OF THE COTTON YARD, 1910. Bidders congregate beneath the roofed structure.

THE 1910 FLOOD. As seen here, the floodwaters covered much of Caldwell Street and Railroad Avenue. The building to the left is James Business College.

HORSE RACING AT THE OLD FAIRGROUNDS, 1910. The fairgrounds were located on 40 acres bounded by Oak, Harkrider, Mill, and Ingram Streets. Governor Donaghey opened the first Faulkner County Fair, which featured horse races (offering a total of $1,260 in prize money), a reunion of the United Confederate Veterans, and a firework display.

THE HOME OF SHERIFF JAMES S. JOHNSON, 1911. Johnson poses with his wife, Minnie, their infant son Carlos, Anna Belle Erbacher (holding the doll), Mildred Groom (the smallest child), and Maude Nation.

THE EDWARD ERBACHER RESIDENCE.

A STREET SCENE, LOOKING SOUTH ON FRONT STREET DURING THE 1914 WATER IMPROVEMENT. Due to past problems with the wooden pipe system, the water works improvement district board and the street improvement board voted to replace the first system with cast-iron water mains before paving the streets with 6 inches of concrete. The former Greeson Drug Store is shown here on the left, the depot is on the right, and an early Frauenthal and Schwarz is in the distant center, along with Cole Grocery.

A STREET SCENE, LOOKING EAST ON OAK STREET FROM FRONT STREET DURING THE 1914 WATER IMPROVEMENT. Contractor Joseph McCoppen installed the first water system, which was made of cypress wood, in 1911. The system was plagued with leaks and pressure problems. Shown in this view, the Terry and Adkisson Mule Barn was located near the present site of the Unpainted Furniture Store. Beyond the mule barn is the Old Grand Theater.

44

THE FRAUENTHAL HOME UNDER CONSTRUCTION, 1915. J. George Chapman was the head carpenter on this building project, which was considered a showplace of the time.

AN UNIDENTIFIED CHURCH ON COURT STREET, 1916. The black community established this church on Court Street. The name of the church is unknown.

A VIEW OF THE FLOOD SCENE AT RAILROAD AVENUE AND OAK STREET, 1920.

A VIEW OF THE FLOOD SCENE AT NORTH AND FRONT STREETS, 1927. On Tuesday, April 19, 1927, floodwaters covered the roads and rails, and disabled long-distance phone lines. Conway's only access to the outside world for two days was a lone Western Union telegraph circuit.

THE I.N. FIELDS FAMILY, 1920. Family members are gathered for a portrait in front of their home at 231 Mill Street.

A VIEW OF FRONT STREET.

RAILROAD AVENUE, 1929. This street was later renamed Parkway Avenue.

FRONT STREET, 1930. A Live & Let Live Sale banner is hanging on the Frauenthal and Schwarz building.

A COTTON YARD, 1930.

A VIEW LOOKING NORTH FROM FRONT AND OAK STREETS, 1930. Notice that the sign reads "Milch Cows Bought Sold and Exchanged."

A View of the Railroad Depot, 1930.

51

FRONT AND OAK STREETS. By 1959 the corner of these two streets had seen many changes.

Four

PEOPLE

Conway citizens have always been passionate about their town. Religion, education, and community were high priorities of early residents. The standards that they set still show in the community and people today.

THE MERRIMAN HOME, 1898. Sam and Minnie Merriman Heiligers are shown standing in front of their home on North Front Street. Heiliger's first grocery store was located at the corner of Oak and Front Streets. Minnie Heiliger was the first president of the Conway School Improvement Association and helped establish the Faulkner County Hospital.

A GROUP OF PROMINENT BUSINESSMEN POSING FOR A PHOTO IN 1890.

THE 1895 CONWAY CITY BAND. The members of the band shown here are, from left to right, as follows: (front row) unidentified and Hugh Pence; (middle row) Casper Dum, unidentified, Bailey Wilson, unidentified, and Ed Shrol (leader); (back row) Henry Erbach, Joe Enderlin, Albert Lachowsky, Phillip Yeager, and August Hein.

MAXIMILLIAN AND PHILOMINA SCHNEIDER.
Philomina Herbert married Maximillian four
months after her fiance, Augustus Schneider
(Maximillian's brother), drowned in Adams
Lake. Maximillian's family came to Conway
in 1873.

THE GREEN GROVE MASONIC LODGE, 1901. Lodge No. 107 met on Saturday night on or
before the first full moon of each month. Lodge members are pictured here, from left to right,
as follows: (front row) Dr. J.H. Matthews, T.H. Russell, D.M. Chivers, J.T. Campell, Dr. I.N.
McCollum, J.T. Harper, Dr. W.R. Greeson, J.M. Campbell, W.B. Brooker, and H.W. Cook;
(middle row) J.R. Suter, J.S. Jones, Dr. G.D. Dickerson, D.L. Paisley, J.M. Oathont, Dr. J.S.
Westerfield, W.N. Owen, W.H. Duncan, W.B. Wilson, and J.W. James; (back row) J.A. Pence,
Sam Frauenthal, J.W. Underhill, H.W. Hoover, J.B. Higgins, and G.W. Chisler.

AN UNIDENTIFIED GROUP POSES IN FRONT OF THE S.G. SMITH STORE, 1910.

A BAPTIST CHURCH SUNDAY SCHOOL CLASS, 1900. Shown here with her class is Sunday school teacher Fannie Dunaway Hogan Goodman. The church is now known as First Baptist.

DR. GEORGE SNYDER BROWN, AN EARLY CONWAY PHYSICIAN. An advertisement in the June 15, 1882 issue of the *Log Cabin* reads as follows: "G.S. Brown, M.D., and G.D. Dickerson, M.D., physicians and surgeons, promised all calls night and day promptly attended to." Dr. Brown's home, built c. 1900, was located at the northwest corner of Caldwell and Center Streets. Dr. Brown died in 1928.

DR. GEORGE DICKERSON RELAXES WITH A JOURNAL IN HIS OFFICE. Dr. Dickerson's office was located on the second floor of the Faulkner County Bank Building on Front Street. This photo was taken in 1910.

WOODMEN OF THE WORLD DRILL TEAM. The Fraternal Lodge of Insurance members posed for this photo in 1910.

WORLD WAR I DRAFTEES FROM FAULKNER COUNTY IN FRONT OF THE COURTHOUSE, 1917.

ODD FELLOWS HALL. The IOOF (International Order of Odd Fellows) Center Line Lodge No. 73 met every Monday night. Dr. A.C. Mattison, Alex Jones, Columbus Blair, Sam Pery, Ben Stewart, Sherman De Vass, Marshall Burton, Claude Eads, Jim Thompson, Jim Jones, Albert Zynamon, John Dorman, and Willie Spann were among the members attending this 1912 social function.

Dr. George Douglas Dickerson and Brothers, 1911. Shown here posing for a family portrait are, from left to right, as follows: (seated) Dr. Preutiss Dickerson and Dr. George Douglas Dickerson, (standing) Rod Cephas Dickerson, Arthur Bill Dickerson, and William Haskill Dickerson.

The Fraternal Order of Woodmen of the World, 1913.

An I.N. Fields Family Portrait, 1915.

Arkansas State Normal College Association Members, 1915. Shown here in front of the Layman's Hotel on Front Street are the following, from left to right: (front row) Harry Ponder?, Dr. A.C. Millar of Hendrix College, John Stubbs, unidentified, Marcellus T. Davis?, and Lee Cazort; (back row) Charles E. Durham, Jo Frauenthal, J.J. Doyne (president of the State Normal School), William D. Cole, G.L. Bahner, J.C. Clark, J.E. Little, S.G. Smith, Henry B. Ingram, J.G. Cubage, and Benjaman Harton.

THE FAMILY OF JOHN D. AND EMMA B. DUNAWAY. John worked as a store clerk and operated a wagon yard; he was also a member of the 1874 Constitutional Convention that framed the Arkansas Constitution and served as a state senator from 1886 to 1890. The John Dunaway family moved to Conway in 1892 to provide their children the opportunity to have a quality education.

THE SONS OF ROBERT "BOB" AND EMILY ADAMS (ROY G., TURNER, ROBERT, AND HARRY). The Bob Adams family home was on the corner of Western and Louvenia Avenue. Bob was a schoolteacher, farmer, and gin owner. He also worked for the sheriff's office and served as a deacon for the First Baptist Church. His parents, Thomas and Ara Adams, arrived in Conway in 1880.

A Chester Allen Markham (Speaker) Family Portrait, 1936. Pictured from left to right are as follows: (front row) Sarah Philips Harrod, Chester Allen Markham, and Mary Josephine Harrod Markham; (back row) Joseph Allen Markham and his wife, Lucibelle Workman Markham; Irene Markham Davenport and her husband, Paul Davenport; and Clara Mae Markham Speaker and her husband, Richard Edwin Speaker. The children are Mary Virginia Speaker, Joseph Allen Markham Jr., Paul Markham Davenport, and Barbara Elizabeth Speaker. The Markham family are descendants of Chester Allen, who was born near Conway in 1875. Markham served as Faulkner County's first sheriff.

The First Methodist Church Businessmen's Bible Class, 1935.

THE OLD SETTLERS ASSOCIATION, 1928. Members are pictured here as follows: 1. Jo Frauenthal; 2. J.A. Mode; 3. I.M. Campbell; 4. A.M. Ledbetter; 5. Ben L. Griffin; 6. Tom Flippin; 7. W.T. Wilson; 8. R.B. McCulloch; 9. Dr. G.S. Brown; 10. George W. Donaghey;

11. J.H. Hartjie; 12. W.D. Cole; 13. Minor Wallace; 14. J.D. Collier; 15. P.H. Prince; 16. W.J. Snow; 17. H.B. Ingram; and 18. Rev. Alex McPherson.

HERMAN STERMER. A licensed HAM radio operator, Stermer worked as the first engineer at KCON radio from 1950 to 1954. He also hosted "Ye Ole Cowpuncher," an early morning radio show. James Clayton founded KCON in 1947.

Five

TRANSPORTATION

Transportation has played an important role in the economy and lifestyle of Conway residents. The biggest impact came with the arrival of the railroad. Passenger rail service linked Conway with large established towns such as Little Rock and Fort Smith, providing a convenient mode of transportation for both business and pleasure.

CORA BLACKWELL AND A FRIEND ENJOY A BUGGY RIDE IN 1900. Miss Blackwell, the daughter of Richard Blackwell (an early pre–Civil War pioneer), was employed at Frauenthal and Schwarz.

RAILROAD TUNNEL CONSTRUCTION, 1903. A convict work crew and spectators stand inside the mouth of the tunnel near its completion.

CHESTER MARKHAM AND FABER HICKS TAKE A BUGGY RIDE, 1900.

Railroad Agent J.W. James. Seen here on the right, James worked alongside four others in the railroad depot in 1905.

AN ADVERTISEMENT FOR THE I.N. FIELDS AND SON WAGON SHOP, 1910.

A LUMBER TRUCK, 1910.

ANDREW J. WITT TAKES A DRIVE IN HIS AUTOMOBILE, 1920. Witt served as Conway's first city recorder in 1875 and as county sheriff from 1882 to 1886. He also worked as a store clerk.

ETHRIDGE'S HORSE AND MULE BARN, MARKHAM STREET, 1910. Heigel's first large delivery wagon is shown leaving the horse and mule barn. Hinkle Ethridge is visible at the far right.

ERBACHER'S MEAT WAGON—THE CONVENIENCE OF HOME DELIVERY.

BEN GWIN, 1910. Gwin is shown driving Hiegel's first small delivery wagon on Oak Street, near the Heigel Lumber Company.

THE RAWLEIGH REMEDIES WAGON. Marvin E. Thomas, a traveling salesman, prepares to pedal his wares in 1920. Thomas ran the service from 1918 to 1922. He carried abstracts, spices, toilet articles, general remedies, and stock and poultry preparations. Farmers and others who lived in remote areas often looked forward to visits from traveling merchants, as they bought needed items and caught up on the latest news.

THE RAILROAD DEPOT, 1923. These men are waiting for the morning train.

THE RAILROAD DEPOT, 1925. Shown here, from left to right, are two unidentified men, Charles Evans, Gray Camp, Charley Newman, Mont Stone, Barker Brown, Floyd Ball, Jamie Anderson, Oscar Sims, Hiram Charles, and George Heit.

A Crowd Gathers at the Train Depot.

BUCK CARTER AND BILL BERRY PREPARE TO BOARD AN AMERICAN EAGLE BI-PLANE (CONWAY'S FIRST AIRCRAFT) IN 1927. Buck Carter was the flight instructor who soloed Berry in 1924. Berry and S. Theodore Smith (Berry soloed Smith) formed a partnership to purchase the plane, which was manufactured in Little Rock. A municipal airport was built along Ingram Street in 1928. Dennis Cantrell (soloed by Berry in 1933) took over operation of the municipal airport in 1946. The airport was later named Cantrell Field in his honor.

TRUCKS AND WAGONS LOADED WITH COTTON BALES ARRIVE AT THE COTTON YARD, 1930.

A Martin Dairy Delivery Truck Prepares to Make Deliveries, 1935. The Faulkner County Dairy Company purchased the Martin Dairy Company in Little Rock and a small ice cream plant in Morrilton in the 1920s, along with several new trucks to service the new area.

World War II Aviation Training. From left to right are William M. Berry, Buck Carter, S. Theodore Smith, Dennis Cantrell, and Kenneth Starnes. The Civil Pilot Training Program was established in 1940 to train some of the 7,000 pilots needed in World War II. Arkansas State Teacher's College provided the ground-school portion of the program.

B.R. Zellner Still Using a Horse and Wagon to Deliver Cotton to the Otis Moore Gin, 1945. The gin, located on Markham Street next to the present site of Fred's Discount, closed in the mid-1960s.

A COTTON WAGON, 1900. This wagon has stopped near the location of what is now Train Station Park. On the far left is the old McNutt building.

TRUCKER FRED FIELDS' 1923 MODEL-T FORD. Fields posed in front of the Clarence Day Feed Store and Grocery Store for this photograph in 1949.

MR. AND MRS. FRED FIELDS, 1950.

ENGINE 8012. On March 28, 1960, this engine became the last northbound passenger train to leave Conway.

Six

WACS and Defense

Arkansas State Teacher's College (now the University of Central Arkansas) was one of seven sites selected as a training camp for the Women's Army Corps of World War II. WAAC Branch No. 3 was activated February 10, 1943, and operated until February 1944.

WACS. Eager to begin training, members of WAC Class 4 arrive in Conway from Georgia on April 9, 1943. Branch 3 WACS were trained to fill out forms for the army. The women filled clerical positions, which freed male soldiers for battle.

WAC Staff, Faculty Officers, and Civilian Officials, February 16, 1943. Included in this group shot is Gov. Homer Adkins. Opening ceremonies for WAAC Branch 3 were held at Estes Field on March 1, 1943.

WAC Class 1, Company A, in front of Old Main, March 1, 1943. The WACS had to

dress in drab, government-issue uniforms. Hats were required at all times while outdoors.

COL. WILLARD H. CRAWFORD. In 1943 Colonel Crawford was commander of WAC Branch 3.

WAC CLASS 2 ARRIVES FROM FT. OGLETHORPE, GEORGIA, MARCH 19, 1943. Young women were eager to participate in the WAC program; it offered opportunities to work in jobs that had previously been reserved for men.

Lt. Osburn Returns Salutes from Students. A staff of U.S. Army personnel was brought to Arkansas State Teacher's College to train the WACS.

WAC Class 2 Arrives in Conway, March 19, 1943. The Bachelor Hotel (Conway's best-known hotel) can be seen in the background. Many community social functions took place at this hotel on South Front Street before it burned on December 31, 1962.

WAC Class 3 Departs from Conway, May 20, 1943. After successfully completing training, WACS were assigned duties at army bases around the country.

WAC Class 5 Arrives in Conway, May 27, 1943. The women followed a regular army regimen from 6:15 a.m. to 5 p.m. daily.

A Dance at a U.S.O. Opening, July 3, 1943. WACS were occasionally allowed to attend dances at Camp Robinson on the weekends.

WAC CLASS 5, LEARNING MILITARY DISCIPLINE, JUNE 9, 1943. The class is taking part in physical training as part of the complete army regimen.

WAC TRAINEES WORK TO ACHIEVE PHYSICAL ENDURANCE, JUNE 9, 1943.

THE CHALLENGE OF PHYSICAL TRAINING, PART OF THE WACS DAILY TRAINING REGIMEN.

WAC OFFICERS ARE SWORN IN, SEPTEMBER 1, 1943.

A 1943 GRADUATING WAC CLASS ON THE STEPS OF OLD MAIN. Twelve classes (a total of 1,200 women) graduated from the Branch 3 training camp.

WAC BRANCH 3, STAFF, AND OTHER MILITARY OFFICERS OBSERVE THE WAC CEREMONY, OCTOBER 22, 1943.

WAC Private Kent, Newlywed of Lt. Earl Kent, Received Notice of Her Husband's Death while Training at Branch 3. She stands at attention as the military ceremony begins in which she will be presented the Distinguished Flying Cross and Air Metal in honor of her husband. The photo was taken in October 1943.

LT. EARL C. KENT, HUSBAND OF PVT.
HELEN G. KENT. Lt. Kent was shot
down over Europe in 1943.

WAC PVT. HELEN G. KENT
STANDS AT ATTENTION DURING
FLY-OVER AT ESTES STADIUM,
ARKANSAS STATE TEACHER'S
COLLEGE, OCTOBER 1943.

WAC Pvt. Helen G. Kent and Col. Todd of the Stuttgart Army Airfield. Pvt. Kent is receiving the Distinguished Flying Cross and the air medal with a three-leaf cluster in honor of her husband.

WAC Private Kent Maintains Military Composure after Receiving Her Late Husband's Medals. Private Kent was later killed (May 13, 1945) in a plane crash in New Guinea.

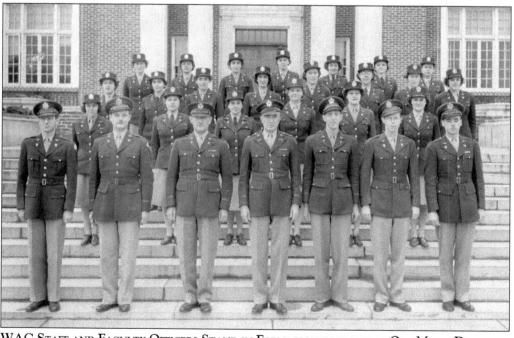

WAC Staff and Faculty Officers Stand in Formation in front of Old Main, December 20, 1943.

A Portrait of Col. George Washington Bruce, 1890. Colonel Bruce, a former Civil War prisoner, was an influential pioneer of Conway. He helped establish Central College (now Central Baptist College) and Hendrix College. Bruce also served as a member of the state house of representatives and for two years as mayor of Conway. He and his wife, Sarah, had nine children. Their home (the first two-story brick home in Conway) was located at the southeast corner of College and Davis Streets. It was razed in the 1980s.

An Army Day Retreat Parade, April 6, 1943.

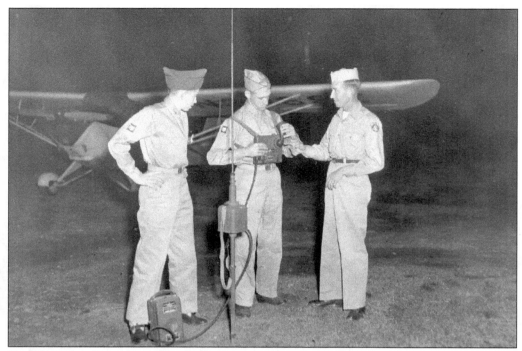

THE CIVIL AIR PATROL IN ACTION, 1950.

MEMBERS OF THE CIVIL AIR PATROL RECEIVING INSTRUCTION, 1950.

Seven

EDUCATION

Education has always been a high priority with Conway citizens. Private schools, public schools, and four colleges have provided children and adults with quality education, thanks to the interest and generosity of prominent business owners and citizens.

THE OLD GREEN SCHOOLHOUSE, 1889–90. This was Conway's first public school. A.P. Robinson donated the property and designed the building, which was located on Locust Street.

A CONWAY SCHOOL PORTRAIT, 1895. This photograph was taken in front of the second white school building. The two-story building was constructed at the corner of Davis and Prince Streets in 1893. Each floor contained four rooms.

THE 1920 CONWAY HIGH SCHOOL GIRLS' BASKETBALL TEAM.

CONWAY HIGH SCHOOL GRADUATES, 1923. From left to right are as follows: (front row) Eunice Morgan, Bernard Glenn, Marguerite Sammons, Turner Adams, W.D. Jeter, Maggie Denison, Clarence Hamilton, Inez Gray, Joe B. McGee, and Maude Payne; (middle row) Mary Collier, Kimbro Brown, Fern Williams, Edith Sims, Mabel Southerland, Ruth Carter, Elwin Burns, Amberdale Lancaster, Montie Snow, Maude Hairston, Mary Burns, and Georgia Harrison; (back row) W.G. Milburn, Mayo Kerr, Ora Day, Pearl McClain, Faber White, Blanche Scull, Myrtle Carpenter, Helen Peacock, and two unidentified men.

THE PINE STREET SCHOOL, 1950. The earliest record of the Pine Street School is 1892, when the Conway Board of Education elected S.P. Marshall teacher. The building pictured was constructed in 1910. The school closed in 1970.

A View of Arkansas State Teacher's College, Facing the Administration Building (Old Main), 1954. This is now the University of Central Arkansas. The college began as Arkansas State Normal College on September 23, 1908, thanks to the generosity of Conway's leading citizens, who rallied to contribute $60,000 needed to construct the first buildings. John James Doyne was selected as State Normal's first president and he presided over the school from 1908 to 1917.

THE 1905 ARKANSAS STATE NORMAL COLLEGE MEN'S BASEBALL TEAM. Coach W.O. Wilson is seated in the center. The first baseball team only participated in competition as a club sport. Season records were instigated in 1916 and the AIC took effect in 1928. That same year the Bears won their first league championship.

THE 1909 ARKANSAS STATE NORMAL COLLEGE MEN'S FOOTBALL TEAM. Normal's first football team finished the year with a 3-3 record. The college received athletic recognition in 1915, when G. Dan Estes took over as head football coach. Third from the left in the back row is coach and professor W.O. Wilson.

A VIEW OF THE ARKANSAS STATE NORMAL SCHOOL'S ORIGINAL BUILDINGS, 1913. The Cordrey Science building is in the foreground and Doyne Hall is on the right. In early years, the science building housed administration, classrooms, an assembly room, and the library.

WOMEN STUDENTS POSE IN FRONT OF DOYNE HALL AT ARKANSAS STATE NORMAL SCHOOL, 1915.

A TYPICAL DOYNE HALL DORM ROOM, ARKANSAS STATE NORMAL SCHOOL, 1915.

AGRICULTURE STUDENTS WORKING IN THE GARDEN AT ARKANSAS STATE NORMAL SCHOOL, 1915.

An Arkansas State Normal School Agriculture Class Working in the School's Garden, 1915.

The Agriculture Class at Arkansas State Normal School during in a Livestock Judging Competition, 1915.

112

HENDRIX COLLEGE, FRONT GATES, 1915. Hendrix College began as Central Institute at Altus, Arkansas, in 1876. In 1890 Conway citizens pledged $55,000 to relocate Hendrix to Conway. Local residents constructed the first three buildings.

HENDRIX COLLEGE STUDENTS, 1910.

A VIEW OF HENDRIX COLLEGE'S ORIGINAL BUILDINGS, LOOKING EAST FROM WASHINGTON AVENUE, 1890. The center building contained the dining hall, classrooms, and offices. The smaller buildings were the north and south dormitories.

EARLY PRESIDENTS OF HENDRIX COLLEGE:
STONEWALL ANDERSON (1902–1910),
ALEXANDER C. MILLAR (1887–1902 AND
1910–1913), AND JOHN HUGH REYNOLDS
(1913–1945).

THE HENDRIX COLLEGE ADMINISTRATION BUILDING. Erected in 1928, this building was destroyed by fire in 1982.

LILY POND AND THE STAPLES AUDITORIUM, HENDRIX COLLEGE, 1950.

OLD MAIN AT CENTRAL COLLEGE. A.P. Robinson donated 10 acres located at the intersection of College Avenue and Center Street to establish Central in 1892. Conway citizens donated buildings to the school. Rev. Charles M. Williams served as Central's first president.

A May Day Celebration at Central Baptist College, 1915.

STUDENTS AT CENTRAL BAPTIST COLLEGE FOR WOMEN IN A MAY DAY CELEBRATION, 1915. The institution was established in 1892 to educate young ladies. The curriculum encompassed first grade through the preparatory department. The college department began with the freshman class and continued with four years of college courses. In 1922 Central became a junior college and was admitted to the American Association of Colleges and Schools, Junior College Division. The all-girls college closed in 1947. The college re-opened under new ownership and became a co-ed campus in September 1952 as Conway Baptist College. The name was changed to its current name, Central Baptist College, in 1962.

CENTRAL BAPTIST COLLEGE FOR WOMEN PRESENTS A FLOAT IN THE 1914 FAULKNER COUNTY FAIR PARADE.

Eight

POLITICS

Politics have been a part of the Conway community since the birth of Faulkner County. When Conway and Pulaski Counties released part of their land to form Faulkner County, it may have been a political maneuver to create political positions of power in the new posts created by the establishment of a new county.

POLITICAL LEADERS OF CONWAY, 1894–1898. From left to right are W.B. Wilson, R.S. Maddox, Judge Rice, Ike Cambell, J.N. Cornell, Edward Erbacher, and H.B. Ingram.

P.H. PRINCE, FAULKNER COUNTY JUDGE FROM **1888** TO **1890.** This photo was taken in 1888.

G.W. RICE, FAULKNER COUNTY JUDGE FROM **1894** TO **1898.** This photo was taken in 1894.

A Group of Men around the First Faulkner County Courthouse, Locust Street, 1873.
A.P. Robinson donated the property on which this structure was built. The courthouse burned in 1890.

THE 1895 GRAND JURY. From left to right are as follows: (front row) J.M. Roberts, J.S. Latimer, L.E. Pearson, W.H. Shannon, D.M. Chivers, E.E. Jones, and J.M. Gentry;

(back row) J.B. Ball, S.S. Wilson, James McLuer, A. Shoulders, Thomas Farris, J.L. George, D.O. Harton, and J.A. Madden.

SENATOR GUY H. MUTT JONES
AND PRESIDENT HARRY S.
TRUMAN, 1950.

A 1958 POLITICAL RALLY FOR
GOV. ORVAL E. FAUBUS ON THE
STEPS OF THE FAULKNER COUNTY
COURTHOUSE. Joe Castleberry,
Bill Sanson, Guy H. "Mutt" Jones,
Charles Acuff, Archie Ford, and
George Hartji Jr. were among the
political leaders in attendance.

A POLITICAL LUNCHEON, 1958.

A FLAG CEREMONY IN FRONT OF THE COURTHOUSE. From left to right are Jack Ward, Joe Castleberry, Bill Purtle, Wendell Bryant, flag presenter J.W. Yoeman, E.A. Calf Dickens, Jerrell Coker, Woodrow Huston, flag receiver Judge Tom Reedy, and Hiram Gillian (holding the flag).

THE THIRD FAULKNER COUNTY COURTHOUSE, 1964. A large addition containing jail cells, courtrooms, and offices has been added to the rear of this building. It is still used today.